When I Had Two Hearts Beating Inside of Me

**JASNOOR
GREWAL-KULAAR**

This book is dedicated to our first-born,
our daughter, Sehheraag Kaur Kulaar.

I couldn't believe I was becoming two.
I knew my world would be happier with you!

I was overjoyed but also cautious, afraid,
trying my best to keep you safe.

Your dad and I wanted to keep you a secret;
we weren't quite ready to announce you yet.

When you were four months old inside my tummy,
we told some we were going to be Daddy and Mummy.

Blessings and cheer rose into the air.
People started asking just who was in there.

But we weren't sure if we wanted to know.
We pondered while you continued to grow.

We decided that it would be a surprise;
a boy would bring sunshine—a girl, the sunrise.

You made my heart go wild, then calm, like the sea.
I realized I had two hearts beating inside of me!

Two hearts—one yours and the other mine.
Joy tumbled up and down my spine.

A smile blazed across my face,
like the soothing breeze of lull and grace.

The weeks ticked by; and it was almost time!
You were soon to be the firstborn of mine.

It wasn't easy, but it was certainly worth it.
The world needed you, and you did deserve it.

You were on my chest and in my arms.
You shone so bright; you were all the charms.

You looked at me with those big, hazel eyes.
You must've felt my keen, cool sighs.

Your fists were delicate like jasmine buds.
Your hair, still wet, was set smooth in little rosettes.

Now you're growing into a beautiful, big-hearted girl,
discovering a wonderful, imperfect world.

Sometimes it goes by way too fast,
but I know memories and moments can last and last.

My heart will forever long for you.
I'll be yours; always there for you.

I'll protect you and love you with glee,
just like when I had two hearts beating inside of me.

ABOUT THE AUTHOR

Jasnoor Grewal-Kulaar is a teacher, writer, new mom, and observer of life's greatest and smallest miracles. She loves nature and travelling. She has taught both children and adults for over six years and is currently specializing and educating in the fields of TESOL (Teaching English to Speakers of Other Languages) and LINC (Language Instruction for Newcomers to Canada).

Jasnoor lives in Edmonton, Alberta, with her husband and daughter. *When I Had Two Hearts Beating Inside of Me* is her first book. She is forever thankful for her husband's and parents' unceasing support in making this book, and her other dreams, a reality.

◆ FriesenPress

One Printers Way
Altona, MB R0G 0B0
Canada

www.friesenpress.com

Illustrations by Tyra Schad

ISBN
978-1-03-916200-6 (Hardcover)
978-1-03-916199-3 (Paperback)
978-1-03-916201-3 (eBook)

1. JUVENILE NONFICTION, FAMILY, NEW BABY

Distributed to the trade by The Ingram Book Company

Printed in the USA
CPSIA information can be obtained
at www.ICGtesting.com
LVHW070817091123
763474LV00003B/19

* 9 7 8 1 0 3 9 1 6 1 9 9 3 *

family.

This book assures us that all emotions are welcome on the parenting journey. Each one is precious and illuminating as the parents and child learn about each other. By embracing our experiences, we can celebrate the little things—like the moment a mother realizes she has two hearts beating inside her, the thrill of announcing that they're expecting to friends and family, and the first time she sees her baby's "fists... delicate like jasmine buds."

Tender, tuneful, and poetic, *When I Had Two Hearts Beating Inside of Me* inspires readers to observe the power and magic of their relationships and to fall in love with every challenging and rewarding moment along the way.

FriesenPress

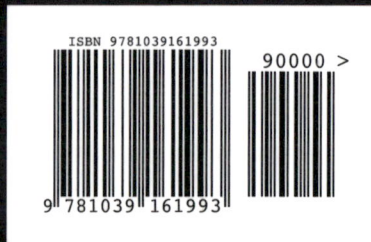

ISBN 9781039161993

90000 >

9 781039 161993